D0202295

FOOTBALL

by
Jane Duden
and
Susan Osberg

CRESTWOOD HOUSE
New York

Maxwell Macmillan Canada
Toronto

Maxwell Macmillan International
New York Oxford Singapore Sydney

Library of Congress Cataloging-in-Publication Data
Duden, Jane.
  Football / by Jane Duden and Susan Osberg.—1st ed.
    p. cm. — (Sportslines)
  Summary: Traces the history of professional football, focusing on the legendary and modern-day heroes of the game.
  ISBN 0-89686-626-2
  1. Football—United States—Juvenile literature. 2. Football—United States—History—Juvenile literature. [1. Football. 2. Football—History.] I. Osberg, Susan. II. Title. III. Series.
GV950.D38   1991
796.332'0973—dc20
                                                                90-26338
                                                                CIP
                                                                AC

J 796.332
DVD

Photo Credits
Cover: AP—Wide World Photos
Princeton University: 4
John Simpson: 6
Harvard University Archives: 7
AP—Wide World Photos: 8, 9, 10, 12, 14, 15, 16, 17, 19, 20, 22, 24, 25, 26, 27, 28, 29, 31, 32, 33, 37, 38, 40, 42
Rice University: 18
Dale Price: 41

Macmillan Publishing Company
866 Third Avenue
New York, NY 10022

Maxwell Macmillan Canada, Inc.
1200 Eglinton Avenue East
Suite 200
Don Mills, Ontario M3C 3N1

CRESTWOOD HOUSE

Macmillan Publishing Company is part of the Maxwell Communication Group of Companies.

Produced by Flying Fish Studio

Printed in the United States of America

First edition

10 9 8 7 6 5 4 3 2 1

Contents

The first college football game: Princeton vs. Rutgers, 1869

Inside Football

Prepare to tackle the game of football! Here's a great lineup of stories and photos. Read about record firsts. Laugh at hilarious fumbles. Learn about superstars past and present. You'll meet record-smashing champions, famous coaches and fanatic fans. They are all in the program, so huddle up for some good reading!

Pigskin Play

At first the game of football looked more like a street brawl. Every kid on the block—or on the prairie—had a different set of rules. Confusion ruled! Punching, scratching, kicking and shoving were all allowed. The players as well as the ball had to be made of sturdy stuff. It was no accident that early footballs were known as "pigskins." Since the game was usually played in the fall, during hog-slaughtering season, the ball was actually a pig's bladder.

The First Huddle Up

It was a contest over a war cannon that led to the first college football match. Two schools, Princeton and Rutgers, were fierce rivals. For years, each claimed the same Revolutionary War cannon. Students took turns making night raids to steal the cannon back from the rival college. Princeton students finally sank the cannon in several feet of concrete. So Rutgers challenged Princeton to the first college football match.

That game, played on November 6, 1869, looked more like soccer than football, since the rules prohibited "throwing or running with the round inflated ball." The players wore no pads, no uniforms, no helmets. They could hit, kick and even dribble the ball to move it downfield. Each kick that went over the goal line scored one point.

Three games were scheduled. Rutgers won the first game at Princeton, 6–4. Princeton won the second game, 8–0. But the third game was canceled. Professors at the schools agreed that the students spent too much time on sports and not enough on studying!

The cannon — sunk in several feet of concrete — that launched football

Clashing styles at the Harvard–McGill game

Soccer + Rugby = Football

In 1874 Harvard invited McGill University of Montreal, Canada, to play a football match. The game would be played on Harvard's home turf in Cambridge, Massachusetts. But a debate arose over the rules. Harvard played football in soccerlike fashion, with an emphasis on kicking. McGill played it rugby-style, catching and running with an egg-shaped ball. Finally, the two teams compromised. One game was played by Harvard's rules, and a second was played by McGill's rules. The game played by rugby rules ended in a 0–0 tie. But Harvard players liked this style so much they adopted it as their own. Soon afterward other colleges in the eastern United States began playing the running, catching and tackling form of football. With a few changes, that 1874 compromise still works!

Pioneer Coaches

As the 20th century began, American-style football took shape. Rugby and soccer were blended together, and American football emerged. Rules were invented. Players were discovered. And coaches became pioneers and legends.

Amos Alonzo Stagg

Amos Alonzo Stagg, the first important American coach, began his career at the University of Chicago in 1892. Over the years, he brought to football the forward pass, the T-formation, the huddle, the tackling dummy and wind sprints. Stagg was forced into retirement at the age of 70. Yet he was so loved and respected that the College of the Pacific in California hired him the year after he retired. He traveled to his new job by train. Also aboard was former United States President Herbert Hoover. "When the train got there," one of Amos's sons remembered, "there were hundreds of people at the station. Amos assumed that they were there to see the president. But they were there to greet him!"

Amos Alonzo Stagg (*center*) with his team

Pop Warner

Pop Warner

Glenn "Pop" Warner was the "father" of the peewee leagues. He brought football to the youth of America. Warner invented plays such as the reverse, the screen pass, and the favorite hidden-ball play. That's when one player stuffed the ball in the back of his teammate's jersey. The player would then jog innocently toward the goal line for a touchdown. It often worked! Warner also devised fiber padding to protect players from injury. And Pop Warner is the reason ball players start every fall practice with the "fundamentals." "You play the way you practice," he said. "Practice the right way and you will react the right way in a game."

Papa Bear

George Halas was one of the founders of the first professional football league, formed in 1920. "Papa Bear" Halas was owner, coach and captain of the Chicago Bears. Halas was 68 when he brought the Bears to the NFL title in 1963. He stopped coaching at age 73. He still holds the record for the coach with the most wins—326 victories.

George Halas

10

Granddaddy of Bowl Games

Imagine a football team beating its opponent, 128–0. Or scoring 501 points in ten games and allowing its opponent *none*! That describes the awesome 1901 University of Michigan Wolverines. People everywhere thought this team was one of the most powerful ever to play football.

In Pasadena, California, the Tournament of Roses Association was planning its annual parade. The group was looking for an exciting event to go with it. With a team like the Wolverines, a football game could be the answer! So the powerful Wolverines of Michigan were invited to play a postseason game against California's Stanford University. The date was set for January 1, 1902, in Pasadena.

The plucky Stanford team played Michigan to a standstill for the first 23 minutes. But then freshman halfback Willie Heston ran 35 yards, and fullback Neil Snow bulled over the line for a touchdown. That was the beginning for Michigan— and the beginning of the end for Stanford. Heston ran 170 total yards. Michigan gained over 500 yards and dominated the second half. The score was 49–0 with eight minutes left in the game. Stanford had six players with serious injuries and no substitutes left. The Stanford captain walked over to the Michigan bench. "If you are willing, sir," he said to Michigan's captain, "we are willing to quit." The captains agreed, and the game was over.

It was such a major defeat that the so-called Tournament of Roses Association Game was not played again until 1916. In 1923 it was renamed the Rose Bowl Game, becoming the granddaddy of all of today's bowl games.

A Killer Sport

Football in its early day was a violent game. In just one year, 1905, 18 college players were killed and over 246 were badly injured. The grab-it-and-run game had no planned plays. Robert Carl Zuppke was a coach for the University of Illinois in the early days of bone-crushing football. He once said to a player, "Son, I don't look for tackles. I listen for them."

After seeing a photograph of a battered college player, President Theodore Roosevelt declared that the game should be outlawed. Some schools, like Columbia, did abandon football. And a special rules committee was created in 1906 to make the game safer. One change was that forward passes became legal. The game took to the air and became more open as players scattered all over the field. The number of yards needed for a first down increased from five to ten. And stricter officiating was encouraged.

Jim Thorpe: All-Around, All-Time Great

Jim Thorpe was one of the greatest athletes of all time. At the Carlisle (Indian) Institute in Pennsylvania, he was a basketball, track and football star. In one football game, Jim ran for

Jim
Thorpe

five touchdowns. He was an All-American halfback in 1911 and 1912. And at the 1912 Olympics in Stockholm, Sweden, Jim became the first Olympic athlete to win both the pentathlon (five track-and-field events) and the decathlon (ten events). King Gustav V of Sweden told Jim, "Sir, you are the greatest athlete in the world."

Like Bo Jackson today, Jim played major-league baseball *and* pro football. Jim's pro football career began in 1915 and ended in 1929, when he was 42! He excelled at every sport he tried, and he tried almost all of them. Jim Thorpe was an all-around great!

Pro Football Kicks Off

At first the public favored the college game and didn't take to the idea of professional football. One early game had only 80 spectators. But gradually that changed. Ohio became the cradle of pro football in America. Canton, Massillon, Akron and Columbus were towns that took football seriously. Interest in pro football spread. Finally, it became a reality. On September 17, 1920, a now-famous meeting took place in a Canton, Ohio, automobile showroom. George Halas later recalled, "We only had two chairs at that meeting. Everybody else sat on the running boards or the fenders." That meeting launched what was later to become the National Football League. Jim Thorpe was elected its first president.

Red Grange carries the ball.

The Galloping Ghost

The 1920s were called the Golden Age of Sports. It was an exciting era, when heroes were made. Baseball had Babe Ruth. Jack Dempsey was hitting hard in the boxing world. And Harold "Red" Grange had become football's unlikely star. Shy and quiet, he came from the small town of Wheaton, Illinois. And he came from hard times. His mother died when he was a young boy. Grange was so depressed that he wanted to quit school. School sports helped Grange through a tough time. And he was good at football. During the summer, Grange would haul 200-pound blocks of ice to help build his strength. The press dubbed him the Wheaton Iceman. Grange was a phenomenal ballcarrier. He could zigzag down the field to escape would-be tacklers. The Galloping Ghost, as sportswriter Grantland Rice called him, signed pro football's first $100,000-a-year contract. In 1925, that was an unbelievable amount of money. He was voted into pro football's Hall of Fame as a charter member in 1963. Red Grange was one of football's first greats.

14

Wrong-Way Riegels

Roy Riegels earned a nickname in the 1929 Rose Bowl that stuck with him for the rest of his career. The center from California had a rare chance to be a ballcarrier in the second quarter. It happened when a Georgia Tech halfback fumbled on his own 35-yard line. Riegels scooped up the ball. He ran briefly toward the Georgia Tech goal. But then he seemed to lose his sense of direction. Turning suddenly, Riegels started for his own goal, 65 yards away. His teammates figured out what was happening and chased after him. They shouted, "Stop, you're going the wrong way!" They finally stopped him two feet from the California goal. Riegels's wrong-way run led to a safety for Tech. Tech won that Rose Bowl game, 8–7. And Roy Riegels was forever after known as Wrong-Way Riegels.

Wrong-Way Riegels holds his head after making a 64-yard run in the wrong direction.

The Big Ukrainian

One rumor said he was so strong that he once knocked over a horse—with a policeman sitting on it! Bronko Nagurski was called the Big Ukrainian. Solid as a rock, Nagurski grew up in Canada. He made his reputation as a fullback at the University of Minnesota. He was a brutal runner and tackler. This steamroller once scored the winning touchdown in a game by dragging six tacklers with him over the goal line! In 1929 Nagurski was named to *every* All-American team.

Bronko played with the Chicago Bears from 1930 until 1937. His Chicago teammate Red Grange recalled, "When you hit Bronk it was like getting an electric shock. If you hit him above the ankles, you were likely to get killed." This pioneer great was inducted into the professional football Hall of Fame when it was created in 1963.

Bronko Nagurski

Football and Thanksgiving

In the 1860s, people played local baseball games on Thanksgiving afternoons. But by the 1880s football games had become the highlight of Thanksgiving for many sports fans. It wasn't long before football became the national Thanksgiving sport. Every year since 1934, the Detroit Lions have played a Thanksgiving Day football game. College and professional football games have become American Thanksgiving Day traditions.

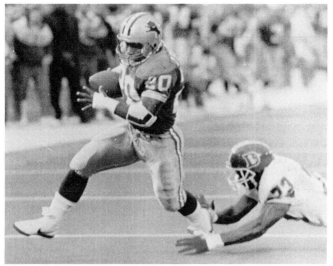

Thanksgiving Day football

Adding Brains to Brawn

Around 1940, the T-formation came into popular use. The offensive backs lined up in the shape of a T behind the center. This allowed them to use many different plays. The T-formation changed the game. Football became a game of brains and strategy as well as muscle. Because of the T-formation, players began to study playbooks as well as pump iron.

17

Platoons in Battle

During football's early days, college athletes wanted to play offense—and defense too. They wanted to block, tackle, run, kick and receive. It was an era of one-platoon football. This meant that all 11 team members played for the entire game. Subs came into the game only if a teammate had an injury or had to attend a class. After 1941, more substitutions were allowed. There just weren't enough players during World War II who could play both offensive and defensive positions. Football "specialists" were born. Athletes who played only one position were recruited. It became a game of two-platoon football. Some football fans would like to go back to the old days when it took all-around versatility to play the game.

A Bench Boo-Boo

It happened in the Cotton Bowl on January 2, 1954. Tommy Moegle of Rice was running with the ball, with no one between him and the end zone. Fullback Tommy Lewis of Alabama was standing nearby on the sidelines. Unable to hold himself back, Lewis raced onto the field and tackled Moegle. His illegal tackle resulted in the referee's awarding Rice a touchdown. Rice won the game, 28–6.

The sideline tackle

Jim Brown leaps for a gain.

Touchdown Maker, Record Breaker

Jim Brown is often called the best running back who ever lived. In 1956 he put on one of the greatest one-man shows in the history of college football. In a single game, the Syracuse All-American broke loose for six touchdowns. And he kicked 7 extra points. His 43 points set the record for most points scored in a major college game. Jim then played pro football for the Cleveland Browns from 1957 to 1966. He wiped the record books clean, then added his own amazing stats. He became one of the greatest touchdown makers, with a total of 126. His career rushing yardage piled up to a record 12,312!

Gaining yards is easier in today's football, and many of his records have been beaten. But Brown is still remembered for his power, speed and brains. As he once said, "The game was my business. My body and my mind were my assets, and injuries were my liabilities." He never gave up, never complained. Brown retired in 1966. And he retired without any serious injuries. He went on to a career in the movies and was a hit in The Dirty Dozen.

The Golden Arm

At first, not too many people thought that Johnny Unitas had a golden future in pro football. Unitas was born in Pittsburgh, Pennsylvania, in 1933. He weighed only a sad 145 pounds at his high school graduation. But Unitas was recruited for college ball by the University of Louisville. Later he was rejected after a tryout with the Pittsburgh Steelers. Unitas didn't give up. He played semi-pro ball for a year, at $7 a game! Finally, in 1956, the Baltimore Colts gambled on Unitas. They signed him with a $7,000 contract. Unitas proved a good investment. He went on to complete more passes for more yardage than anyone to that date in football's history. During his years as quarterback, Unitas led the Colts to one Super Bowl win, three NFL championships, and one American Conference title. Johnny Unitas became the man with the golden arm.

The Golden Arm fires a pass.

The Greatest Football Game Ever Played

Unitas may be most remembered for his role in what is often called the greatest football game ever played. The Baltimore Colts were pitted against the New York Giants in the 1958 NFL Championship. With only two minutes on the clock, the Colts trailed by three points. The Colts were in possession on their own 14-yard line. Unitas, cool as a cucumber in the huddle, told his teammates, "This is where we find out what we're made of." Unitas threw four quick passes and brought the Colts to within field-goal range. It was up—and good! The score was tied, 17–17, as the final gun sounded. The game would be decided in a sudden-death overtime period. How cool would Unitas stay? Did he really have "ice water in his veins"? Apparently so. Unitas rifled several passes to march his team to the New York 1-yard line. The ball was snapped for the last time and fullback Alan Ameche shot across for the winning touchdown. It was a golden victory for the man with the golden arm.

Big Bucks, Small Potatoes

Football has not always been a well-paid job. Instead of big bucks, most players in the early days signed for small potatoes. In 1957 the salary ranges looked like this:

Cleveland Browns:	$6,000–$19,000
Chicago Bears:	$6,500–$14,200
San Francisco 49ers:	$5,600–$20,000
Green Bay Packers:	$5,000–$18,500

Playing pro football nowadays is big business. Today's

big-name football pros ask for—and often get—huge sums. Some salaries are in the millions. How much should a player be paid? Will there ever be a limit to pro football salaries?

The Money Wars Begin

When the American Football League (AFL) was formed in 1959, many NFL officials were upset. They had been the pioneers, and they resented the new league. But the players felt differently. They liked the new league. Why? Their salaries soared as the two leagues bid against each other to sign the best talent available. The "money wars" were on, and a bitter NFL-AFL rivalry had begun.

Golden Boy

It wasn't just his golden hair that earned Paul Hornung his nickname, the Golden Boy. He knew how to score. In early December of 1960, he broke the old scoring record of 138 points for a player in one season. Two weeks later, on

Paul Hornung picks up a couple of yards.

December 17, he brought his season's point total to a record 176. Hornung scored a fourth-quarter touchdown. He followed that with his fifth extra point of the day. The Golden Boy did more than set the record for most points in a season. He also led the Green Bay Packers to their first divisional championship in 16 years.

Phantom Fan

Avid fans often imagine themselves playing with the pros. One football fanatic did more than just imagine. It happened in Boston on November 3, 1961. The Dallas Texans (now the Kansas City Chiefs) were one touchdown behind the Patriots. It was time for the Texans to fire up. They tried hard with a 70-yard pass to Chris Buford, but he landed flat under three defensemen on the 3-yard line. With that, thousands of Patriot fans ran onto the field to celebrate. The referees shooed them away. They said there was time for one more play.

No one noticed the extra man in the Patriot secondary. A Patriot fan had lined up among the Patriot defenders. Dallas quarterback Cotton Davidson sent a pass to Buford in the end zone, but the ball never got there! The Patriot fan leaped into the air and deflected the ball to the ground. Just then, the final gun blasted, and the fan disappeared into the crowd. The Patriots had won the game. None of the officials had noticed the fan's leaping interference. Davidson, though, was hopping mad. He got even madder when no one believed his story. Luckily a film of the game later proved Davidson right. The out-of-uniform fan had made a great play for his team. To this day, no one knows the identity of that phantom fan.

Vince Lombardi on a victory ride after the 1968 Super Bowl game.

Toughest Man in Pro Football

Vince Lombardi had a reputation. He was head coach of the world-champion Green Bay Packers from 1959 until 1967. Lombardi is famous for saying "Winning is not everything. It is the only thing." What did people say about this grinning, growling, winning coach?

Joseph Lombardi (younger brother of Vince): "My brother can beat your father."

Sid Gillman (fellow coach): "He does what everyone else does—only better."

Alex Wojciechowicz (fellow player): "He was ready to kill himself to win."

Bart Starr (Packers' quarterback): "I owe my life to that man."

Max McGee (Packers' wide receiver): "He's the most egotistical man I've ever met."

This legendary coach died of cancer in 1970 at the age of 57. His own words sum up his career: "You never lose. But sometimes the clock runs out on you."

Running Wild!

On December 12, 1965, a soft-spoken rookie halfback went on a scoring binge that tied a 36-year-old record. Gale Sayers of the Chicago Bears scored six touchdowns in one game. He scored on runs of 80, 21, 7, 50 and 1 yards. Then he returned a punt 85 yards for his sixth touchdown. That matched the number of touchdowns scored by two other players: Ernie Nevers of the Chicago Cardinals against the Bears on Thanksgiving Day 1929 and Dub Jones of the Cleveland Browns, also against the Bears, in 1951. After the game, Sayers was awarded the game ball. That made another record: He became the first player in Bears history to be awarded two game balls in one season.

Gale
Sayers

25

Coming Together

By the 1960s the NFL and the AFL had become bitter rivals. The two leagues tried to outbid each other for the best football players. If these bidding wars continued, both leagues would go broke.

In 1966 the NFL and the AFL agreed to merge, forming today's National Football League (NFL), with two conferences. The leagues were to play separate schedules until 1970. Following the 1966 regular season, the top team in each conference would meet in a championship game that came to be called the Super Bowl.

Super Bowl I

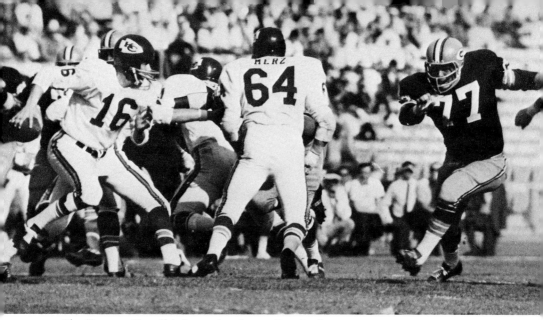

The Kansas City Chiefs vs. the Green Bay Packers

Super!

Bounce . . . bounce . . . *boing* . . . bounce. Sharon Hunt liked to bounce her small red, white and blue ball over the roof of her house. She told her dad it was a super ball.

Sharon's dad, Lamar Hunt, was the owner of the Kansas City Chiefs. It was the year 1966, and Mr. Hunt had the championship game between the NFL and AFL on his mind.

"In our discussions we kept referring to it as the 'final game' or the 'championship game' or whatever, but it was awkward." One day Mr. Hunt came out with, '. . . when we get to the Super Bowl . . .'" The name stuck. Football's official Super Bowl name came from Sharon Hunt's super ball.

Super Bowl I was played between the Green Bay Packers (representing the NFL) and the Kansas City Chiefs (AFL) on January 15, 1967, at Memorial Coliseum in Los Angeles. Green Bay won, 35–10.

27

TV and Monday Night Football

In 1970 Howard Cosell, "Dandy" Don Meredith and Keith Jackson brought Monday night football into millions of living rooms on television. Today football is the most watched of all American sports. The popular TV program marked its 20th season in 1990. Announcers have changed over the years, but one thing stays the same: The players all want to do their best in front of the TV cameras.

Howard Cosell (*center*) with fellow announcers Don Meredith (*left*) and Frank Gifford.

Pump 'Em Up

Football takes strength and muscle. Some players spend a lot of time in the weight room to build bulk and speed. But one of the most effective muscles for a middle linebacker like Dick Butkus was his "levator labii superioris alaeque nasi."

Dick Butkus

Actually, this is a very small muscle. It is the muscle that lifts your lip into a sneer. Dick Butkus of the Chicago Bears used that muscle a lot. He was a bear of a man at 245 pounds. He usually looked grim, grouchy and ready to get you. And Butkus could back up his sneers with king-of-the-hill assaults that flattened his opponents. Quarterbacks feared him. "The best way to play Dick Butkus," one said, "is to avoid him." That was hard to do. Butkus loved to hit. He was a ferocious tackler. He held the defense together with his mulelike strength and animal instincts. Some claimed that Butkus *was* the defense.

Dick Butkus came into the league in 1965. By the end of that first year he had won All-NFL honors as a middle line-backer. It was an amazing feat for a rookie. Knee injuries forced Butkus out of the game and into retirement in 1973. But he scared the socks off more than a few players before hanging up his own cleats.

Pick a Number. Which Number?

Can a football player pick any number to wear on his jersey? Nope—not since 1972, when the National Football League ruled on a number-by-position policy. To find your favorite players and their positions, look for these numbers:

Quarterbacks and kickers: 1–19
Running backs and defensive backs: 20–49
Centers and linebackers: 50–59
Other linemen: 60–79
Tight ends and wide receivers: 80–89

The Comeback Kid

As a kid, shy Joe Montana stayed around home a lot. His best friends were his mom and dad, along with a few neighborhood kids. He would play ball in his backyard with his father, then come in to eat his favorite meal: a plate of his mom's ravioli. Montana was an all-around good athlete. He had played spring baseball and football since the age of eight in the peewee leagues. But Joe Montana always said that his favorite sport was basketball. "I could practice basketball all day," he says. Practicing football, he claims, was *work*.

Montana is a modern-day quarterback legend. After high school, he signed with Notre Dame. That's where he earned the nickname the Comeback Kid. Montana would be called off the bench in the fourth quarter with seconds left on the clock. His team would be trailing. And Joe Montana would torpedo the ball into the waiting hands of his receiver. It always baffled the other team to see Montana's "mondo" drives downfield.

Joe Montana

Scores were made in the final gun's blast. The win would be stolen away by Montana's easy-as-pie aerial attack.

Then came the famous "chicken soup" game. Notre Dame was matched against Houston in the 1979 Cotton Bowl. Dallas had been hit with a freak storm, and ice covered the stadium and the field. Montana was suffering from a dangerously low body temperature. He had to be led to the locker room and covered in blankets. The shivering Montana was fed hot chicken soup to warm him. In the meantime, Houston had forged ahead, 34–12. With less than eight minutes left on the clock, Montana ran back onto the field. A roar went up from the crowd. Joe fired three perfect bullet passes to rally his team for a win. The final score: 35–34.

Fans doing
The Wave

The Victory Wave

You're munching your popcorn and balancing a soda pop on one knee. Someone starts The Wave. Sure, you're a good fan. You'll join the sea of fans as they rise, wave their arms in the air and yell for your team. The wave creates a sonic boom of sound sure to raise your team's spirits.

The wave mania began at the University of Washington in the mid-1970s. Unfortunately, it backfired. The fans were so loud that it cost the home team five-yard penalties. Their own offense muffed several plays in the deafening roar. Michigan Coach Bo Schembechler begged his fans to play the wave somewhere else. But thanks to television, the wave caught on all around the country.

O. J. on the Run

"*Thinking* . . . is what gets you caught from behind," according to O. J. Simpson. He has been called the best pure runner of all time, a player who *feels* his way down the field. "Once through the hole, I usually know where the strong safety is coming from, even if I can't see him. I just know where he *should* be."

O. J. hurtles down the field.

Orenthal James Simpson grew up in the Potrero Hill section of San Francisco. He knew where he should be and where he wanted to be. O. J. Simpson wanted to play for the team he watched as a teenager—the San Francisco 49ers.

As a boy, O. J. had watched Jim Brown rush for record yardage against the 49ers. After the game, O. J. collected seat cushions from the stands. He turned them in for a nickel each. O. J. was at the ice-cream store to spend his money when Jim Brown walked in. "You just wait till I get up there," Simpson said. "I'll break all your records."

That boyish wish later came true. After winning the Heisman Trophy in 1968 at the University of Southern California, O. J. was drafted by the Buffalo Bills as a running back. His best season was played in 1973. Going into the final game of the year, he needed 61 yards to break Jim Brown's single season rushing record of 1,863 yards, set ten years earlier. It was the Bills against the Jets in New York, and a snowstorm was raging at Shea Stadium. But O. J. knew where he should be and wanted to be. Churning up 200 yards, Simpson broke the record.

He finished his football career with the San Francisco 49ers in 1978–1979, having gained a total of 11,236 rushing yards. Today O. J. performs in a different arena—commercials, sports announcing, TV and movies.

The Last Time Woody Lost It

He was a great coach, and his temper tantrums made him even more of a legend. Woody Hayes, the Ohio State football coach, could have given a two-year-old lessons in head banging, punching and foot stomping. Once in frustration he bit his own hand hard enough to draw blood. And Woody's was not the only blood drawn: He hit camera operators. He tore up sideline markers. He made referees wish they had chosen another line of work.

Woody, though, was often forgiven. He could win games as well as lose his temper on the field. With 13 Big Ten titles, O.S.U. could put up with Woody's mischief. But that changed at the Gator Bowl on December 29, 1979. National TV showed Woody Hayes attack an opposing player. Poor Charlie Bauman of Clemson. He had intercepted a pass along the sideline, dooming O.S.U.'s chance to win. Charlie didn't know Woody would be waiting for him. The coach drove through Charlie's throat with his thick forearm. Then Woody's players took their own chops through pads and helmets when they tried to hold the old coach down. O.S.U. said that enough was enough, and Woody Hayes was fired the next day.

City Limits

Grand Island took great pride in being the third-largest city in the state of Nebraska. That is, until 1981. That's when University of Nebraska fans filled Memorial Stadium in Lincoln, Nebraska, to watch the school's home football games. So many "Go Big Red" rooters filed in to watch their Cornhuskers that the stadium became the third-largest "city" in the state! Move over, G.I.!

A New Kind of RICE?

Playing football and other sports means sore muscles—and sometimes injuries. Today's players try RICE. The RICE used by sports pros and trainers everywhere stands for Rest, Ice, Compression and Elevation. Here's how it works:

Rest: Stop the activity as soon as you can.

Ice: Apply ice. It will limit the swelling and allow the injury to heal much faster.

Compression: Try a light wrap with an elastic bandage around the injury to prevent swelling and provide support.

Elevation: If your arm or leg is injured, lift it onto something higher than chest level. Gravity helps limit the accumulation of fluids and decreases swelling.

The Dream Team: Fantasy Football

Are you tired of your favorite team losing? Do you wish you could have a say about which players are on the team roster? Imagine being the general manager of your own football team. That's what you do when you play Fantasy Football. Books came out in the 1980s on how to play this game. Now sports fans all over the United States are playing out their dreams. They create their own teams made up of actual NFL players. They memorize statistics. They scout the college prospects and try to draft the best players. They watch regular games during the football season and read the newspapers to see how their players did. Scores are tabulated. Winners brag and losers weep, just like in the big time.

Bo Knows

Bo may not know diddly, but Bo does know baseball. Bo knows football and Bo knows track. Vincent Edward Jackson, known as Bo Jackson on playing fields, knows sports. The 6 foot 1, 230-pound athlete has run the 100-meter dash in 10.1 seconds. In 1985 he won college football's top honor, the Heisman Trophy. He set a single-game rushing record of 221 yards for the Los Angeles Raiders in 1987. As a leftfielder for the Kansas City Royals, he hit 32 homers in 1989. Bo went on to earn baseball's All-Star Game's MVP award in July 1989.

Bo Jackson in action

Payton's final game

The Man Called "Sweetness"

His mom wanted help with the chores around the house. One son, Eddie, was already on the football team, and he had no time. So it was Walter who came home after school to help. There was no football for Walter Payton until his sophomore year in high school. That didn't stop him from charging his way into the record books. Walter Payton became the greatest running back in history. By the end of his tenth pro season, in 1984, Payton had broken Jim Brown's career rushing total.

A remarkable man called Sweetness, he had a gentle manner and a lilting voice. After 13 seasons with the Chicago Bears (1975–1987), Payton retired. He had gained more rushing yards than any other player in pro football history: 16,726. He also holds the record for most career 100-yard games: 77. Payton was such an admired player that his jersey number, 34, was retired at his final home game at Chicago's Soldier Field on December 20, 1987. As he walked off the field for the last time, 66,000 loyal fans watched. They chanted in farewell, "Wal-ter. . .Wal-ter." He was 33, a young man but an old runner.

Who Gets Hurt?

Football players keep getting bigger, faster and stronger. The game is getting rougher at all levels, from high school to the NFL. As a result, the field of sports medicine does more than repair injuries. It tries to prevent them in the first place.

The National Athletic Trainers' Association (NATA) wants to make sports safer. One way the organization does that is by learning which players get hurt and when. In 1988 about one-third of all high school football players were injured. Sixty percent of the injuries happened during practice rather than during a game. For every 100 games played, NATA learned who gets hurt:

8.3 injuries are to running backs

6.6 injuries are to quarterbacks

4.6 injuries are to defensive linemen

4.4 injuries are to wide receivers

4.3 injuries are to linebackers

3.1 injuries are to offensive linemen

2.7 injuries are to tight ends

2.7 injuries are to defensive backs

Most players feel that the rewards outweigh the risks. Boston Patriots quarterback Steve Grogan is one. "Football teaches a lot of great values: discipline, teamwork, confidence—so many things you can apply to life that you don't learn unless you're part of a team working toward a common goal. If you train and condition and study the game, you lessen the risk of being hurt." So go for it—but play it safe!

It Beats Catching Bricks

On January 22, 1989, Jerry Rice played the kind of game most players only dream about. Jerry caught 11 passes for 215 yards (a Super Bowl record) and one touchdown. The San Francisco 49ers beat the Cincinnati Bengals, 20–16. It brought the 49er wide receiver his biggest sports thrill—being named the Most Valuable Player of Super Bowl XXIII.

Jerry Rice receives the MVP award.

One of the best pass receivers in pro football got his start catching bricks. As a teenager, Jerry and his older brother, Tom, spent summers carrying bricks to their father, a brick mason. To make a tough job easier, Jerry and Tom tossed the bricks between them. Jerry's catching hands were extraordinary. But it was Jerry's fast feet that got him into football. One day during his sophomore year in high school, he was standing in the hall when he should have been in class. The principal walked up behind him. He scared Jerry, who took off running. When the principal finally caught up with Jerry, he told him to report to the football coach. The rest is history.

Jerry was named All-Pro in 1986 and every year since. In 1987 Jerry set a league record by catching 22 touchdown passes, and he was named the NFL's Most Valuable Player.

But the 1989 Super Bowl was Jerry's dream come true. Then in 1990, the 49ers won the Super Bowl again. Jerry's three touchdown receptions set another Super Bowl record.

A Crown for the Kicker

How can a homecoming queen help win the big game? It's not so hard if she's the team's placekicker! Tamara Browder was the 1989 homecoming queen at Woodward High School in Toledo, Ohio. Tamara was crowned homecoming queen at halftime while wearing her football uniform. During the game, Queen Tamara kicked two extra points to help her team win, 14–0. That's one homecoming queen who earned her crown!

Homecoming Queen Tamara Browder: Congrats from Dad

41

Not for Guys Only

"You're a girl—you can't play. Football is too tough." Have you heard these words? Cheerleaders are not the only females on the football field these days. Girls in America's backyards everywhere are trying football plays with their neighbors and friends. Some have gone on to play in organized mixed leagues. At some high schools, a boys' team may have a female placekicker. Women like tennis pro Billie Jean King and former first lady Betty Ford enjoyed playing football as young girls. Linda Jefferson, a professional football player for the Toledo Troopers, says, "Although football is a rough sport, there is nothing to fear because you play against girls your own size. Football is a wonderful challenge, and you get a sense of unity when playing on a team." So if you're a girl and want to play an exciting game, huddle up!

Women in the Locker Room?

In October 1990, Sam Wyche, the coach of the Cincinnati Bengals, got slapped with a $30,000 fine. Why? Wyche had refused to allow a female reporter to enter the Bengals' locker

Reporter Barry Turnbull (*left*) and Coach Sam Wyche (*right*) spoof the locker-room tiff.

room after a game. He insisted, "I will not allow a woman to walk into a room of 50 naked men." Instead, Wyche sent a player outside the locker room for the reporter to interview. But the NFL rules say that locker rooms are open to all official reporters. The NFL fined Wyche the largest sum ever for a coach.

Reading the Play, Loud and Clear

The cheers from the crowd. The crashing of helmets. The groans from the players. We *hear* football as well as see it. But not Ken Walker, a senior defensive tackle with the University of Nebraska in 1990. Deaf since the age of two, Ken Walker plays football without the sound. And he plays it well. So how does Ken know what play is being called in the hurdle? The team's defensive captain stands face-to-face with Walker and speaks clearly. Walker reads his lips. Teamwork pays off, in the classroom as well as on the field. Ken has a sign-language interpreter with him for his classes at the university, where he studies art.

Football Timelines

1869: Princeton and Rutgers play the first organized football game.

1892: William "Pudge" Heffelfinger, an All-American guard from Yale, becomes the first known professional football player.

1899: A neighborhood football team on Chicago's south side is formed by Chris O'Brien. This team eventually becomes the St. Louis Cardinals, making it the oldest continuous pro football club in history.

1920: The American Professional Football Association (APFA) is formed. Jim Thorpe is elected president.

1922: The APFA changes its name to the National Football League (NFL).

1926: The first American Football League (AFL) is formed, in direct competition with the NFL. It folds in 1927.

1929: A fourth official is added to pro ball. A field judge now officiates along with the referee, umpire and head linesman.

1930: The first NFL night game is played.

1931: The first All-Pro team—the best of the best—is selected.

1933: Official statistics are kept for the first time.

1936: The first organized draft of college players into the NFL is established.

1939: A football game is shown on television for the first time.

1940: NFL football is first broadcast on radio.

1943: All football players are required to wear protective helmets.

1953: Willie Thrower joins the Chicago Bears, becoming the first black quarterback to play in the NFL.

1956: A radio receiver is first used by coaches on the sidelines for calling plays to their quarterbacks on the field.

1959: The American Football League is formed again. Founded by Lamar Hunt, it begins play in 1960.

1961: George Blanda of Houston throws 36 touchdown passes. He sets the record for more touchdown passes in a season than any player in pro football history.

1963: The pro football Hall of Fame opens in Canton, Ohio. To be inducted is the highest honor a pro football player can achieve.

1967: New York Jets quarterback Joe Namath passes for more than 4,000 yards in a single season. It is an NFL first.

1970: The NFL and AFL are combined into one league called the National Football League. Two separate conferences, the AFC and the NFC, now make up the NFL.

1970: The longest field goal in NFL history is kicked by Tom Dempsey of the New Orleans Saints. He kicks the ball an amazing 63 yards.

1971: The first modern Pro Bowl pits all-stars from the NFC against those from the AFC.

1971: Alan Page of the Minnesota Vikings becomes the first and only defensive lineman in NFL history to be selected as the season's Most Valuable Player.

1973: The NFL adopts the system of numbering jerseys by position.

1975: The World Football League folds after only two seasons.

1979: Steve DeBerg of the San Francisco 49ers beats Fran Tarkenton's pass completion record of 345, tossing 347.

1982: NFL players go on strike. Some players return after two months, and a modified football season is played out.

1983: Dallas Cowboy Tony Dorsett makes the longest run from scrimmage in NFL history. Dorsett shocks the Vikings with a 99-yard run.

1984: The San Francisco 49ers win 15 of their 16 regular-season games. It is the most victories in a single season in league history.

1986: The first NFL game ever to be played in Europe takes place between the Chicago Bears and Dallas Cowboys in London, England.

1986: Dan Marino of the Miami Dolphins beats his own NFL record of pass completions in a season with 378, 16 more than the NFL record he set in 1984. His 623 passes are the most ever thrown by an NFL quarterback in one season.

1987: Dallas Cowboys star Herschel Walker becomes the tenth NFL player in history to reach the 2,000-yard mark in one season.

1990–1991: NBC signs a deal to pay Notre Dame University almost $38 million to televise the home games of the Fighting Irish. Is college football, like pro football, becoming big business?

Index

48